LIVING WITH DICKENS

LIVING WITH DICKENS

Tom Bianchi

ST. MARTIN'S PRESS, NEW YORK

ACKNOWLEDGMENTS

I thank the following people for their contributions to the making of these photographs and this book:

Tony Casale • Michael Denneny, my editor • Albert Fleites and Lola Karen Gillis • Robert L. Green • Keith Kahla • Doris Borowsky Nathan Chandler Keith and Whitney • Del Kolve • Larry Luchtel Arthur Roger and Bambi • Jaye Zimet. Special thanks to Elfrieda Chay, whose love for Ingrid and Dickens opened me to a better understanding of them, and whose care for us all enhances our lives. And Larry Laing, whose professional printing talent has made these photographic prints beautiful. I especially thank Mark Prunty, my partner. His imagination, wit, critical advice, and effort is on every page of this book.

ISBN 0-312-08765-9

First Edition: January 1993

10 9 8 7 6 5 4 3 2 1

FOR OUR MOTHERS

Bambi/Dickens' Mother

Ingrid

FOREWORD

Like many people who are deeply involved in meaningful relationships with cats, I was raised with dogs, and for years considered myself a dog person. The cat in the house I grew up in was a Siamese named Chelsea. She belonged to my sister. I never bonded with this creature, whose expression of affection toward me was the occasional deposit of a lizard tail on my pillow. I did not realize my capacity to appreciate a relationship with an independent-minded creature until 1985.

In the spring of that year, I met a kitten named Ingrid Ermine. With large brown spots on a white coat, she appeared to me as a pleasant cross between a Palomino pony and a panda. The first time I saw her, she seemed to be "digging for China" in a flower pot. Admiring her industry, and having no luck with house plants, I brought her home. She settled in and chewed through enough bamboo to confirm that she did, indeed, have panda in her.

Ingrid was a high-energy cat. For the first two years of her life, I was determined to keep up with her. Gradually, however, I tired of hide-and-seek, paper-ball soccer, and catch-me-if-you-can. Also, we had moved into a town house, the back of which is a wall of glass looking out on a common garden. I feared that I might cause my new neighbors concern if they noticed me frequently on all fours, at all hours, ducking behind various pieces of furniture. As I became a less playful partner, Ingrid slowed down, too. My Palomino panda kitten evolved into a Holstein. Since I had determined her universe—the inside of our house, me, and an occasional insect—I felt responsible for enriching her environment. I decided to find her a companion who could pep things up.

Enter Dickens. In November of 1987, *Connoisseur* ran a cover story on the "Cat of Cats," Abyssinians, which were described as gorgeous and fun-loving. Perfect—I thought. This cat could live up to the name I decided any future addition to our family would bear—Ukute Little Dickens—a name my grandmother called each of her twenty-one grandchildren. In early December, I received a serendipitous visit from an art dealer from New Orleans, Arthur Roger. He had a pair of Abyssinians, Bambi and Pogo, who had just produced their first litter. Arthur called them Kibbles and Bits. (I must interject here that most cats have the ability to transcend baby names with regular demonstrations of dignified and elegant behavior. On balance, however, I think it makes more sense to have a Bambi who can enter a room with grace than a Lady Astor who chews her hind claws in public.) As Arthur told me about these kittens, I knew the one he described as fearless was Dickens. Dickens was about to meet an extraordinary challenge.

Ukute Little Dickens

I must explain what this eight-week-old kitten had to deal with. Ingrid is extremely territorial. While she views me as a lap opportunity, she welcomes visitors with the warmth Elizabeth I gave the Spanish Armada. She much prefers a guest's purse or coat to the guest's person. Many friends have left this house with an "Ingrid the Terrible" tale. Anyone, for example, who has presumed that a chair Ingrid is occupying might be available to themselves, has quickly discovered Ingrid's frightening snarl, which means, "Listen, buster, this isn't Siegfried and Roy. I don't jump off chairs on command."

Obviously, since this book is titled *Living with Dickens*, he was up to the challenge. I arranged to have Dickens flown from New Orleans to Los Angeles. Although I feared that he would arrive traumatized, Dickens emerged from his carrier and immediately demonstrated that his first and primary instinct was to play. On his first encounter with Ingrid, he announced with his own hiss that he was now top cat.

Dickens took Ingrid's growl and hiss as an invitation to play a game of "Me cougar, you Holstein." Ingrid, to my relief, seemed to enjoy the mayhem in the house, taking up Dickens' games with enthusiasm. She initiated regular bouts of "Speed Cat and Thunder Paws," dropped a few pounds, and returned to her former svelte self.

With me, Dickens' games have been more subtle. He quickly established who was to be teacher. Early on, he taught me "Throw." Cats don't fetch. If he deems your throw inadequate he will sit and stare at you until you retrieve the toy and throw it far enough to satisfy him. I have often watched him bring a toy to the foot of a guest, leaving me to explain the rules of the game.

His most common conversation with me is a tiny meow which I have come to understand means "No one is playing with me." This message is usually delivered in the studio with the deposit of a toy on whatever project is absorbing my attention. If I don't respond to his invitation, he reaches up for a rub and a pet. If I remain preoccupied, he wraps his paws around my leg and bites me. Things rarely escalate this far, as I've learned well my function in his life.

Over Dickens' five years of life, he has been the star of the show in our house. Dickens has gotten top billing because he pretty much charms his way into getting everything he wants. Both Ingrid and I have come to terms with this. He greets our guests, especially the ones who think they are allergic, with a nuzzle (his breed is known for seducing people who don't like cats), keeps the toilet paper monster at bay, and has taught us all to be more sharing—especially with food—specifically with him.

The camera, to Dickens, is another cat toy, a signal that he will now get my undivided attention. This fortunate circumstance has allowed me to make this record of our lives together. He is graced with that singular quality I find and admire in beings who are possessed of great and true beauty—the ability to toss repose aside in an instant for the sake of having fun.

On His Zebra Throne

Art/Yawn

Who's Ernie?

Oh No, the Vacuum Cleaner

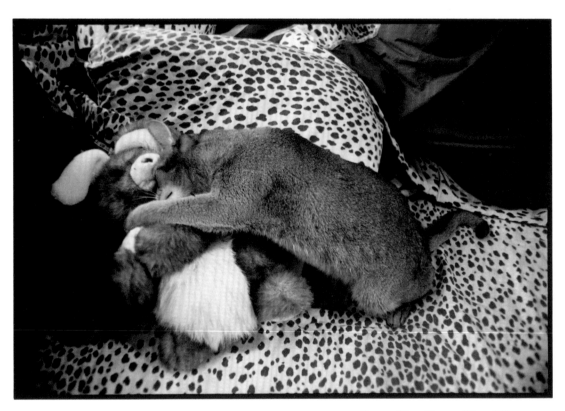

Love You/Love You Thumper

Just Bacon, Thank You

My Honey Bear

In the Closet

Anywhere But His Water Bowl/1

I N G R I D—Where Are You?

My Closet! My Closet!

Toilet Paper Monster

Hi There

Love My Polar Bear

Kill My Polar Bear

Head Shots

Rorschach Cat

Poolside Portrait

Now This Is Art

Just Take the Picture

Love You/Love You Lamp

My Hurrell Portrait

Love High Places

Rich Cats

My Grass!

Bad Boy

Whitney Spots the Thief

If I Could Fly

I'm Not Starting Anything

Lola Comes for a Visit

Dickens, the Host from Hell

My Lunch?

A Whiff of Silk

Aaah

Choo!

My Potato Chip

Where the Treats Are

Cover Cat

A Little Catnip Between Friends

Nature Cat

Top Cat

No More Pictures!

~~Tom and Dickens~~
Dickens and Tom